PADDLE YOUR OWN CANOE

OR

TIPS FOR BOYS

From the Jungle and Elsewhere

By

LORD BADEN-POWELL
OF GILWELL, O.M.

Chief Scout

Copyright © 2013 Read Books Ltd.
This book is copyright and may not be
reproduced or copied in any way without
the express permission of the publisher in writing

British Library Cataloguing-in-Publication Data
A catalogue record for this book is available from the
British Library

Robert Baden-Powell

Robert Baden-Powell was born in Paddington, London in 1857. After attending Rose Hill School, Tunbridge Wells, Baden-Powell was awarded a scholarship to Charterhouse public school. Here, he was an enthusiastic outdoorsman, gifted pianist, and talented actor. After graduating, in 1876, Baden-Powell joined the 13th Hussars in India.

Baden-Powell was soon transferred to the British secret service. As an agent, he frequently travelled disguised as a butterfly collector, incorporating plans of military installations into his drawings of butterfly wings. After three years as intelligence officer based in Malta, at the age of 40, he was promoted to lead the 5th Dragoon Guards in 1897.

During the 1880s and early 1890s, Baden-Powell had began to write in earnest, producing a number of military books: *Reconnaissance and scouting* (1884), *Cavalry Instruction* (1885), *Pigsticking or Hoghunting* (1889), *The Downfall of Prempeh* (1896) and

The Matabele Campaign (1897). In 1899, Baden-Powell penned a small manual entitled 'Aids to scouting'. A summary of lectures he had given on the subject of military scouting, it was aimed at helping train recruits.

Baden-Powell returned to South Africa prior to the Boer War and was engaged in a number of actions against the Zulus. Promoted by the time of the Boer War to the rank of colonel, he oversaw the famous siege of Mafeking, during which his garrison repelled a Boer army of in excess of 8,000 men for 217 days using various unorthodox tactics. Promoted to Major-General, Baden-Powell became a national hero in Britain.

In 1903, after organising the South African Constabulary, Baden-Powell returned to England to take up a post as Inspector General of Cavalry. Upon his return, Baden-Powell found that his military training manual 'Aids to scouting' had become something of a best-seller, and was being used by teachers and youth organisations. Following a meeting with the founder of the Boys' Brigade, Sir William Smith, Baden-Powell decided to re-write 'Aids to scouting' to suit a younger readership, and in 1907 held a camp on Brownsea Island for 22 boys of mixed social background to test out some of his ideas. *Scouting for Boys* was subsequently published in 1908 in six instalments.

From this point onwards, boys began to spontaneously form scout Troops, and the scouting movement was born, first as a national, and soon as an international obsession. Baden Powell decided to retire from the Army in 1910 on the advice of King Edward VII, who suggested that he could better serve his country by promoting scouting. Over the next three decades he produced a vast amount of books on scouting, including *Yarns for Boy Scouts* (1909), *Aids To Scoutmastership* (1919), *Scouting and Youth Movements* (1929) and *scouting Round the World* (1935).

Baden-Powell was made a Baronet in 1922, and was created Baron Baden-Powell, of Gilwell in the County of Essex, in 1929 – Gilwell Park being the International scout Leader training centre. He was appointed to the Order of Merit of the British honours system in 1937, and was also awarded 28 decorations from foreign states. By 1939, the number of registered Scouts was in excess of 3.3 million, in more than fifty countries.

After suffering from bouts of illness, in 1939 Baden-Powell moved to a house he had commissioned in Kenya. He died here two years later, in 1941, aged 83.

FOREWORD

I WANTED a title for this book that would sum up what is at the back of these stories of the wild animals of the jungle and people of many lands.

It amounts to a very old piece of advice—that you should always try to rely on yourself and not on what others can do for you.

There are plenty of old sayings that might help this lesson to stick in your minds. People used to say, for instance, "Every tub must stand on its own bottom," or in Scotland "Let every herring hang by its own head."

But we don't want to think of ourselves as being either tubby or fishy, so I have fallen back on a phrase very familiar to all Scouts: "Paddle your own Canoe."

FOREWORD

It does at any rate suggest that we are getting ourselves along by our own efforts, taking a few risks, and having a lot of fun by the way.

BADEN-POWELL.

Paxtu
Nyeri, 1939.

CONTENTS

		PAGE
1.	OBSERVATION AND DEDUCTION. Ants as Detectives	1
2.	SELF-EDUCATION. How to learn Geography .	8
3.	ON NOT BEING A SILLY ASS. The Ass-trologers	14
4.	COMMON SENSE—and how it built a Bridge .	18
5.	RESOURCEFULNESS. Pioneering Pygmies . .	24
6.	ENDURANCE. Arctic Explorers . . .	31
7.	ON BEING ACCURATE. Hippos; and the Importance of a Hair's breadth . . .	38
8.	PATIENCE. Don't be in too much of a hurry .	44
9.	GRATITUDE. It may save you from a Snake-bite on the nose	48
10.	COURTESY—as shown by Car-drivers . .	52
11.	GOODWILL—in Rhinos and Elephants . .	56
12.	HONOUR. Whacking the Goat . . .	64
13.	KEEPING YOUR NERVE—even when Rhinos galumph	68
14.	COURAGE—of Lions and Lion-hunters . .	74

CONTENTS

		PAGE
15.	KEEPING YOUR PECKER UP. Bravery against Odds	82
16.	HUMOUR. A lesson from Algernon	88
17.	DON'T SWANK—or you may have to live in a Rabbit-hole	94
18.	ON "STICKING IT OUT" in a drain-pipe	99
19.	HOW TO BE FIT. Lessons from men and beasts	104
20.	THE DUTY OF SERVICE, and how to Be Prepared	122
21.	HELPFULNESS—taught by an Elephant	131
22.	RESPONSIBILITY—learned in a Scout Patrol	138
23.	SELF-SACRIFICE. Heroes of the Antarctic	144

OBSERVATION AND DEDUCTION

Ants as Detectives

"Hi! Stop Thief!" shouted old Blenkinsop as he rushed out of his little store near the Kaffir village. "He's stolen my sugar. Stop him."

Stop whom? There was nobody in sight running away.

"Who stole it?" asked the policeman.

"I don't know, but a whole bag of sugar is missing. It was there only a few minutes ago."

A native police tracker was called in—and it looked a pretty impossible job for him to single out the tracks of the thief from among dozens of other naked footprints about the store. However, he presently started off hopefully, at a jog-trot, away out into the bush.

PADDLE YOUR OWN CANOE

In some places he went over hard stony ground but he never checked his pace, although no footmarks could be seen. People wondered how he could possibly find the spoor. Still he trotted on. Old Blenkinsop was feeling the heat and the pace.

At length the tracker suddenly stopped and cast around, having evidently lost the trail. Then a grin came on his face as he pointed with his thumb over his shoulder up the tree near which he was standing. There, concealed among the branches, they saw a native with the missing bag of sugar.

How had the tracker spotted him? His sharp eyes had descried some grains of sugar sparkling in the dust. The bag leaked, leaving a very slight trail of these grains. He followed that trail and when it came to an end in the

bush the tracker noticed a string of ants going up a tree. They were after the sugar, and so was he, and between them they brought about the capture of the thief.

Old Blenkinsop was so pleased that he promptly opened the bag and spilled a lot of the sugar on the ground as a reward to the ants.

I expect that he also patted the tracker on the back for his cleverness in using his eyes to see the grains of sugar and the ants, and in using his wits to see why the ants were climbing the tree.

Any ordinary person, who had not been taught tracking, would never have noticed these bits of " sign ".

That's where the Boy Scout's training comes in.

OBSERVATION AND DEDUCTION

I have known another case of ants being useful, in fact they were not only useful but saved the lives of several men.

These men were a party of scientific professors who were hiking in the wilds of Australia, searching for rare plants and animals, reptiles and bugs.

Out in the desert they ran out of water. For hours they struggled on, maddened with thirst and weak with exhaustion; it looked as though, like many explorers before them, they would collapse and die. Luckily, to their great relief, a small native girl appeared. They made a sign to her that they were dying of thirst and wanted her to go and fetch water.

In reply she pointed to a string of ants which were climbing up a baobab tree. (This

tree has a great fat hollow trunk which thus forms a sort of water tank.)

The little girl picked a long stalk of dried grass and climbed up to a little hole in the trunk which the ants were running into. She put one end of the straw down this hole and the other end into her mouth and sucked up water.

In this way the wild little imp of the desert taught the learned gentlemen a valuable

OBSERVATION AND DEDUCTION

bit of knowledge which with all their school and college education they did not possess.

I hope that had a Scout been with them he would have been wise to the idea, or at any rate would have used his eyes and wits and would have noticed the ants at their work and guessed why they were using that hole in the tree.

SELF-EDUCATION

How to learn Geography

Where is Kenya?

THE kitchen-maid, in the celebrated play called "Cavalcade", kept asking people—"Where *is* Africa?" and when the cook didn't know she asked the butler, who had served as a soldier in the South African war. He could only explain—"I don't know *where* it is but I know it is blurry hot when you get there."

Well, I don't suppose most people are as ignorant as all that about Africa, but it is astonishing what a number of people don't know where Kenya is. Yet it is an important bit of our British Empire, twice as big as England, and one where many British people now make their homes, as probably some of you who read this will be doing some day.

SELF-EDUCATION

So I hope you will look it up in the map of Africa and not be so dolefully ignorant about it as some of the people who write to me. Every mail brings me letters addressed to "Kenya, South Africa", or West Africa, or Rhodesia, or Gold Coast.

One kind friend told me it must be nice for me to be *so near* to my son Peter. Peter is in Southern Rhodesia, and Southern Rhodesia is over 1,200 miles from Kenya—as far as Albania is from London.

Another hoped I would see her son who is "near Kenya in Sierra Leone". When she was told that the distance between them was pretty long she said—"That's all right, he has got a motor-bike!" (Sierra Leone is about 4,000 miles from Kenya as the cock crows—I mean as the crow flies!)

PADDLE YOUR OWN CANOE

A lady in England said she had a friend living " somewhere between Nairobi and Lake Victoria ". That sounded as though she really knew something of geography, but she went and spoiled it all by adding—" By the way, is that anywhere near the place called Kenya that so many people are talking about ? "

I had a letter this week from the head of a big school in England addressed to me in " Kenya, South Africa "—the two countries being 2,000 miles apart.

So how can a boy be expected to know geography if his teacher doesn't know any better than that ?

But it tells you one very useful thing, and that is that you should not depend altogether on what is taught you in school. The teacher can't teach you everything, but when you have

SELF-EDUCATION

been shown by him how to learn useful knowledge it is up to you to go on and learn things *for yourself.*

The fellows who teach themselves are the fellows who get on in life. Now teach yourself from the map over the page where the different states are in Africa—especially Kenya, on the Equator, where it should be " blurry hot " but isn't.

Now I'll give you a tip. I passed my exams in Geography because I was able to draw maps from memory, and how do you think I did that? Well, when studying a map I used to try and make a face or a figure out of it. In this way I could always draw its outline from memory.

Now look at the map of Africa as I have made it into the head of a girl with spectacles

PADDLE YOUR OWN CANOE

on. Try and draw it exactly as I have done and you will always be able to draw a map of Africa from memory.

The eye of the girl is Lake Victoria, and the arm of the spectacles is the Equator; her forehead is Kenya, her ear is Nigeria; the tears on her cheek are the great long lakes of Tanganyika and Nyassa; her nostril is the Zambesi river-mouth, her mouth is Beira (the port of Southern Rhodesia).

By studying the map you will know where you should insert countries like Ashanti, Northern and Southern Rhodesia, Sierra Leone, the Union of South Africa, etc. etc.

That's one way of teaching yourself geography. So teach yourself and don't wait to be taught.

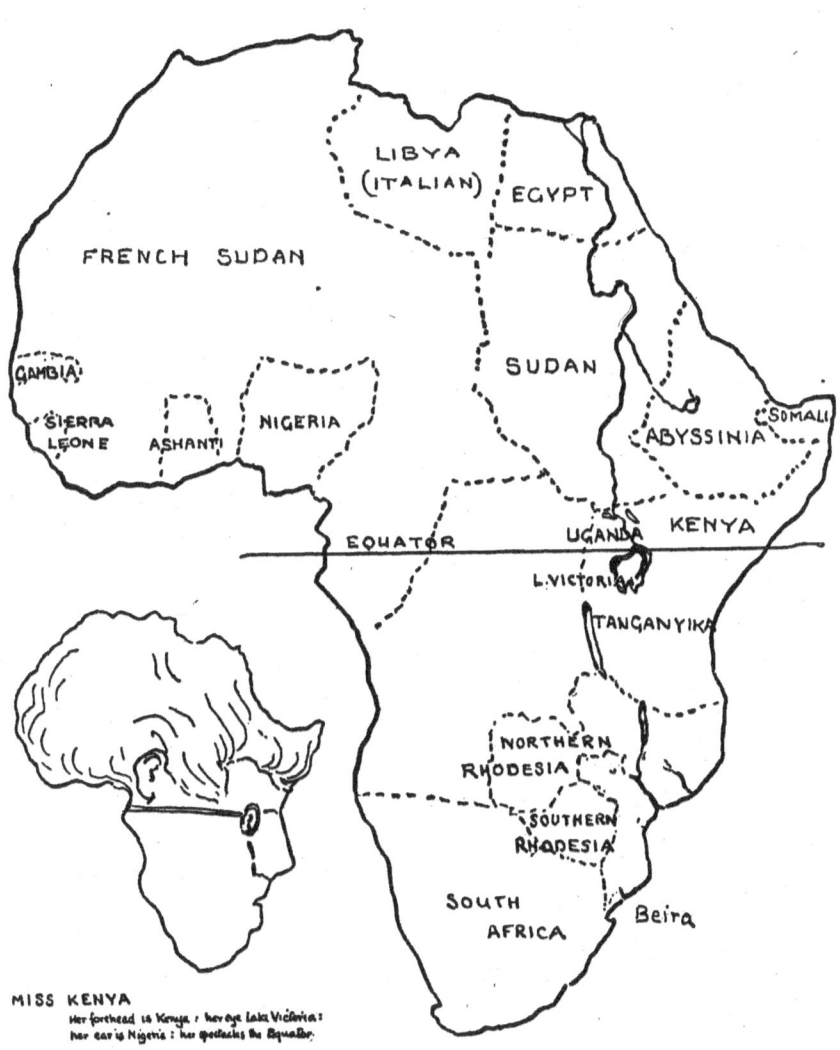

MISS KENYA

Her forehead is Kenya; her eye Lake Victoria; her ear is Nigeria; her spectacles the Equator.

ON NOT BEING A SILLY ASS

The Ass-trologers

I THINK I have written before about the S.S.A., or Society of Silly Asses. It seems to be going ahead like Billy-o in England. A whole lot of people seem to have become members of it—though I don't suppose any Scouts have. Well, they couldn't, if they carry out the eleventh (unwritten) Scout Law which says "A Scout is not a fool".

The people I am referring to are those who believe that their doings, or their luck, can be told by the stars.

The blokes who tell them what the stars say are called "Astrologers", a fine, high-sounding title, and some of these do actually study astronomy; but a whole lot of them are fakers and make up yarns which they hope

ON NOT BEING A SILLY ASS

people will believe and will pay them fees for the information. It is easy to see which are the humbugs if you ask two or three different astrologers for their reports about you when you give them the date of your birth.

When the answers come in no two will be alike. One will say something like this—" Since you were born when the planet Mars was in the ascendant you will be bitten by a dog next year but will recover." Another will say —" Your birthday star tells me that great danger awaits you in the street next Thursday if you go out. Better stay at home all day." And the third will point

PADDLE YOUR OWN CANOE

out that through being born on that date you will receive a large sum of money when you least expect it.

But all three are alike in one thing—they will all expect sums of money from YOU for the valuable information they have managed to get out of the stars for you.

They are wonderfully clever at getting people to believe their piffle, especially dear old ladies and young men who like to be thought a bit different from others. These pretend to be superstitious and to touch wood lest their luck should fail; they won't walk under a ladder—not for fear of the painter dropping paint on them but because it would bring them bad luck. As for the number thirteen, they wouldn't sleep in a cabin or hotel room with that number on the door.

ON NOT BEING A SILLY ASS

No fear. Not they! Nor would they sit down as thirteen people to dinner. The first to leave the table would be sure to die within a short time if they did.

Personally I rather like the number thirteen, partly because it is the number of my Regiment, the 13th Hussars, and, as it happens, over and over again thirteen of us dined together in the Mess, while we were as a Regiment particularly lucky in the matter of deaths.

No. It is only weak-minded people who take up these silly superstitious ideas.

A Scout won't do it if he remembers the Eleventh Law.

COMMON SENSE

And how it built a Bridge

I HAVE just been drawing a picture here of a tall cotton tree which has fallen across our little trout stream. It is a beautiful spot in thick tropical jungle and we often go there for a picnic.

When we get near the spot we sound our motor horn and when we are walking through the bush we talk loudly and even shout to each other. This is not because we are deaf but in order to warn other gentry in the forest that we are there.

The other gentry are rhinoceroses (what a word to spell) and if they are warned that people are about they prefer quietly to sneak away. If we went quietly we should probably come on one of them, suddenly perhaps, in

COMMON SENSE

the middle of his afternoon nap, and he would be startled and alarmed and angrified and come at one with his nasty great horn. When he is annoyed he is just like a motor-lorry driven by a blind driver.

But it isn't about rhinos I want to talk—beyond warning you to use your common sense in dealing with them.

I expect that some of you who read this will one day take to colonial life and have to deal with a rhino or two.

No. It was about that fallen tree that I wanted to talk. It reminded me of a bridge-building feat in West Africa long ago. This was again a case of using one's common sense.

Common sense is almost the most useful and valuable thing you have got in your character. The pity of it is that so few fellows know this or make use of it! They prefer to be guided by what they see written in books instead of using their own wits.

Well, now—about that fallen tree in West Africa. We had come across a very narrow but very deep and rapid river which our own column would have to cross. ("We", I may say, were the advance party of Scouts and Pioneers making the road ready for the troops which were marching a few days behind us.)

The engineer with me made plans, to scale, of a timber bridge for crossing the river, according to the directions in the book of instructions for bridge-building. What with cutting the timbers and fitting them together, preparing rope lashings, telling off working parties with tools, the erection of that bridge

COMMON SENSE

was going to take two or three days or more.

I wanted to get my Scouts across without delay. So I did what I expect a Boy Scout would do—I did not use a book of instructions but I used my common sense. I estimated the width of the river as 100 feet. Then I looked for a tree of that height standing near the bank. Almost at once I spotted the tall branchless trunk of a cotton tree 150 feet high. At him with axes! Cut him in such a way that he fell smack across the stream. In a few minutes my Scouts were trickling across and within half an hour the axemen had shaved off the top side of the trunk to make a flat footpath and had rigged up a bamboo handrail and so established a perfectly sound one-way bridge.

Two days later our army arrived at the river. The Engineers' bridge was not quite ready, so the Army had to content itself with filing across our more humble kind of highway. [Triumph No. 1 for C.S. (Common Sense).]

A few months later the column returned from its expedition. A day or two before it

COMMON SENSE

reached the river on its homeward march there was a tremendous rain-storm. The river rushed down in flood, a mighty torrent which lifted the Engineers' bridge and smashed it up and carried it away in a thousand small pieces. The flood flowed over our C.S. bridge, but when the waters subsided next day there stood our old tree-trunk as firm as ever. A new handrail had to be rigged, but that was the work of a few minutes.

So when the Army arrived a day later they were once more thankful to use our humble but sound way of crossing.

RESOURCEFULNESS

Pioneering Pygmies

SUPPOSING you had a narrow deep river to cross, in which there were lots of hungry crocodiles, but where there were tall trees on both banks, how would you cross it?

You say—cut down a tall tree and fell it across it and so make a bridge. Quite right. So would I. I've told you how I did it. *But*—supposing you had no axe or saw—nothing better than a pocket-knife. What then?

Well, that is just the problem which the Pygmies have to face.

The Pygmies are a race of very small men, only about four to five feet high. They live in the deep forests of the Congo territory, just north-west of Kenya. They are a very uncivilised little people and are nomads, that

RESOURCEFULNESS

is to say they seldom stay long in one place, and when they have shot down the game in their neighbourhood with their tiny bows and arrows and have cleared off all fruits and roots that are good for food they move on somewhere else to new pastures.

This week a friend of mine has returned from visiting them, and has shown me some of their clever handiwork in making their bows and arrows, etc. And he told me about their bridges.

You see, that country is traversed by numbers of small rivers, deep and rapid. The Pygmies can't swim, nor could you if you lived there. You can't learn to swim unless you bathe, and in that country if you go bathing you never come back because the crocodiles get you. The rivers swarm with them.

To build a boat takes a lot of time and is

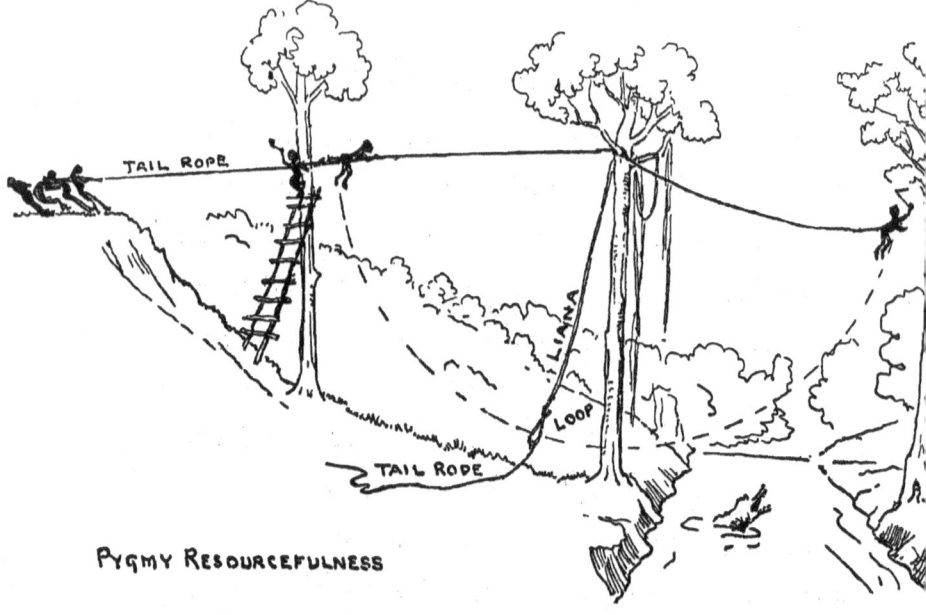

PYGMY RESOURCEFULNESS

hardly worth the trouble just for crossing such small rivers.

But these Pygmies are ingenious little imps and they have got their own way of making a bridge. Of course it would be simple to hack down a tree, but they have not got axes, so they have got a dodge for making a flying bridge which I'm sure would appeal to every pioneer Scout.

RESOURCEFULNESS

Look at the sketch and see if you couldn't make one.

The forests of the Congo are full of tall trees, and hanging from them there are immensely long creepers or lianas. These are as tough and flexible as ropes.

To start a bridge the head builder selects the tallest tree he can find on the bank. He gets a liana long enough to reach across the river, fastens one end of it to the tree-top and makes a loop in the other end as a sling to carry him, clear of the ground. To this sling he ties a tail-rope.

The other Pygmies tail on to the tail-rope and get on to the high ground above the bank of the river and haul away until they have pulled the man in the loop so far back that his main rope is almost horizontal. Opposite the sling, when the rope is tight like this, a ladder is set up and a fellow with a knife climbs to the top of the ladder. On the word "go" he cuts the tail-rope from the loop, and the man in the loop swings away with a hair-raising swoop right across the river. He holds in his hand a big hooked stick and with this he catches on to a branch of a tree on the opposite bank. There he makes fast the loop end of his rope.

Other Pygmies climb along this rope across the river, each bringing the end of another liana with him. Thus in a short time there are a dozen ropes across. With these a good rope bridge is quickly made by which the whole tribe can safely cross.

But it is rather a case of cruelty to animals because down below there, in the river, poor

RESOURCEFULNESS

crocodiles are looking up with their mouths watering, all bitterly disappointed at not getting the meal they had been hoping for.

These Pygmy pioneers give a good example of resourcefulness, that is, of making other things do when you haven't got the things you need for your job.

For instance, elephant chops and steaks are luxurious food for them, but they have not got rifles for shooting the animals, so they make their bows and arrows and raw-hide bow-strings and put a little deadly poison on the arrow-tips. Then they creep up close to an elephant, shoot a little arrow into him, and though he runs off for miles, irritated by the pricking of the arrow, they trot along on his track until he falls and dies. Then the whole tribe have a tuck-in, such a tuck-in that they

PADDLE YOUR OWN CANOE

don't need food for four or five days afterwards!

I could give you dozens of instances of resourcefulness in many different lines—but here is another to illustrate making things do.

I once took charge of a small native boy wounded by a stray bullet and I told his mother to fetch water quickly. She ran off to a stream some distance away, but having nothing in which to carry the water she was resourceful enough to fill her mouth full and brought it back in that way. It turned out to be a most useful substitute for first-aid appliances, as the water was warmed and she could squirt it into the wound, where I cleaned it with a feather, and between us we made a good surgical job of it without any proper first-aid outfit.

ENDURANCE

Arctic Explorers.

You fellows at home had an awful winter this year.

Out here in Kenya it was difficult for us to picture your blizzards and your floods, your fogs and your rain, when only four days away from you by air we were rejoicing in hot sunshine, strawberries, and roses.

PADDLE YOUR OWN CANOE

You must have felt, after such a winter, that you knew pretty well what Arctic explorers have to put up with.

Our Scout ship "Discovery" must have felt quite in her element again and will probably have dreamed that she was back in the Antarctic once more, instead of moored off the Thames Embankment in London.

Your winter, after all, will only have lasted a couple of months. "Quite long enough too," you'll say. Yes, but think of, say, Captain Scott's exploring party. Six of them were landed on an island, with a very small supply of provisions, as the ship was expected to return shortly to pick them up again. But blizzards and ice prevented her, and there they were stuck for *eight* long months, in filthy

bitter weather, with nothing to eat but seals and penguins. Jolly!

Were they downhearted? Not they. At any rate they had discovered this new island and they had to give it a name. But all the names they thought of were too bad to appear in print on a map. A neighbouring island had been named "Inaccessible" Island; so in the end they called theirs "Inexpressible"

PADDLE YOUR OWN CANOE

Island. And thus it stands in the charts to-day.

Gales and blizzards kept on blowing almost all the time, and they were not in a comfortable house with plenty of food and fires to keep them warm. Can you picture it?

Yet, like true Scouts, they kept up their spirits and could "whistle and smile" in spite of bad times, just as you would do.

Half the party were told off to hunt for food, and they killed fifteen seals and 120 penguins and put them in "cold storage" in the ice, for from April to July no birds or animals were to be seen.

The other half of the party made their igloo. This they did by making a tunnel ten yards long in the hard snow, with a living-chamber at the end of it. And that was their

ENDURANCE

home for eight months. They made a thick carpet or mattress of seaweed all over the floor, and found that this really kept them warm. Their kitchen range was an old oil-tin, fed with seal blubber and fuel; and, until a chimney was devised, the smoke, which was more soot and oil than smoke, nearly choked the cook and inhabitants of the igloo.

Among other gadgets invented by these Arctic Scouts was a boat made by covering the bottom and sides of their sledge with canvas soaked in oil to make it waterproof. It made a very good little boat, but in the rough weather of those parts they had not much opportunity of using it.

And remember that another worseness of their winter over yours was that most of the time they were in darkness. No gas, no electric light, but by melting down seal's fat they made oil, and out of an Oxo tin they made a lamp with a wick made from shoestring, and so had an oil lamp to lighten their darkness.

Like Scouts they made numbers of other gadgets and kept their spirits up in spite of all their hardships.

After all they were Britons.

In the end their ship called in and took them off, none the worse for their long exposure, and brought them back to sunshine and civilisation.

So, too, you are soon relieved from the gloom and chill of winter by the sunshine and warmth of summer. After clouds the sun shines again. Whether your particular cloud is

ENDURANCE

sorrow or pain or anxiety the sunshine of happiness will come back to you again if you make the best of things when times are bad.

ON BEING ACCURATE

The Importance of a Hair's Breadth

WHEN I was a boy at school I was stuck into the Cadet Corps. I was very small for it but I could blow a bugle. So I began as a bugler.

I did not imagine that I should ever become a General (though somehow I did so in the end) but I did look forward to being a full Cadet and having a rifle of my own. When that happy time arrived I was very fond of my gun and did my best to shoot straight with it.

Well, " shooting straight ", as any of you know who have practised rifle shooting, means that you have to take most accurate aim if you want to hit your target. If your foresight is the breadth of a hair off the bull's-

ON BEING ACCURATE

eye your bullet will be the breadth of a hand off it.

Some fellows can never get the patience to practise over and over again until their eye can see accurately. They seem to slam off their shot with the idea that the rifle will put it there, and if it doesn't, well, it is the fault of the rifle if they miss.

You remember the fuss I made about shooting a hippo long ago (when the natives gave me the name of 'Mlalapanzi'.) I watched that old hippo for a long time hiding himself under the water but coming up to breathe every two minutes; only his nose and ears appearing above the surface and only for two seconds, but always in the same place.

I had to hit him in the eye. Anywhere

else the bullet would only bang against his great thick skull and do him no harm.

My natives and those in the neighbouring kraal were almost starving, so it was all-important that I should kill that hippo and get his meat for them.

I did not dare to risk a shot from the shoulder when he bobbed up. It would be too hurried for accuracy. So I lay down on my back as the steadiest position for shooting, and had the grass in front of me carefully cleared away. When Mr. Hippo put his head up I took careful aim, in the short two seconds available, at his eye—and a precious small eye it was. But I didn't fire. I kept that aim steadily on the spot where his eye had been and when he came up again I made sure that it was directed straight on his eye;

ON BEING ACCURATE

but again I did not fire. The instant he appeared for the third time I pressed the trigger, and in that second the hippo was dead.

So the natives called me " The man who lies down to shoot", that is, the man who makes his plans carefully beforehand, aims steadily for what he wants to get, and then shoots straight for it.

But that matter of being able to take accurate aim got me into the very useful way of being accurate in other things.

For one thing it helped to give me a good start in the Army. It was this way. With a number of other young officers I was being tested in surveying. Oh yes, you have to know a lot of things in the Army.

We had to take an angle with our compass to a certain spot, and from there to another

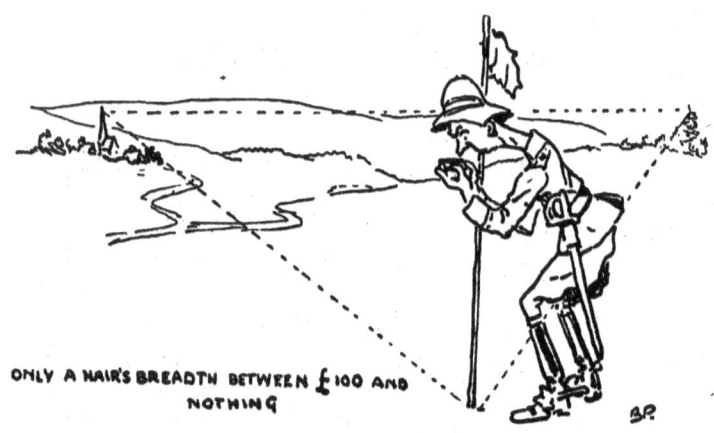

ONLY A HAIR'S BREADTH BETWEEN £100 AND NOTHING

point, and from there to a third point. If one did it correctly this last angle should land one exactly at the spot whence we started.

But it meant extreme care in taking the angles. If you mis-read your compass by the thickness of a hair you would fail to do it.

Only one of our party had been accurate enough to succeed, and who do you think that was?

Little me!

As a result of this and a few good marks in other subjects I got promoted with two

ON BEING ACCURATE

years' back pay, with which I was able to buy the best horse I ever had.

All this through observing to a hair's breadth, if it's only in throwing darts or practising with a miniature rifle.

Once you have got into that habit you will be accurate and exact in all things. Exactly on time and punctual. Neat and exact in your clothing. Accurate in keeping your accounts or your registers in your office; accurate in your work as an engineer, electrician, cabinet-maker, or whatever kind of work it is; and accurate in all that you say.

Remember that accuracy will pull you through to success where others, less careful, fail.

So practise accuracy all you can until it is a regular habit with you.

PATIENCE

Don't be in too much of a Hurry

SHOOTING wild animals with a camera is far better sport than shooting them with a gun. For one thing you have to get much closer to them, and this means more careful and clever stalking—and of course when you are dealing with dangerous animals it is bound to be a bit more hair-raising and exciting.

PEEP BO!

PATIENCE

Now there are two kinds of stalkers. The European is generally too eager to get to his prey; he stalks in rather a hurry, and consequently often startles his animal before he gets near enough for his purpose. It takes a photographer dozens of attempts before he gets a good picture.

The native hunter, on the other hand, will creep and crawl and stand frozen or lie still for hours on end—for a whole day if necessary, but he keeps on and on. The great thing is that he uses patience—and it's through patience that he gains success.

Just like a fisherman. You see a huddled-up figure sitting in a boat hour after hour, through rain or shine, or creeping on hands and knees to throw a fly over a fish without being seen by him. Well, it is only by infinite patience that those fellows get their fish.

Then the fisherman  has a gaudy time when the wind or a bush catches his line and twiddles it up into a hopeless tangle. The ordinary man would curse it and try to disentangle the mess with a determined wrench, only to find that he had got it knotted in a worse jumble than ever. But the true fisherman will know that the only way is to set to work slowly and carefully to trace out the right threads and get them to separate themselves, and though it may take a terrible long time he gets "All Clear" in the end.

PATIENCE

Again it is "Patience" wins the day.

Somewhere I have written—"More careers are ruined by want of patience than through drink or crime."

I have seen so many fellows chuck their job just because they get bored with it and angry with their employer or disappointed with ill-success of their efforts, when if they had quietly whistled to themselves that good old song "Wait till the clouds roll by" and had *made* themselves carry on their job they would in the end have made a success of it.

But no, they chuck it up in a huff and then wonder why they never get forrarder in life.

Everybody—you yourself included—is bound to meet with disappointments and annoyances from time to time, but you will get over them all right if you just pinch yourself and say—"Patience".

GRATITUDE

It may save you from a snake-bite on the nose

"THE honey-bird's a funny bird"—so says the poet. And it's true. He is a little chap, not much bigger than a sparrow, but, my word, he is clever.

He has a way of finding out where the bees have made their honey and he loves honey as much as a boy loves chocolate. But his difficulty is to get at the honey when the bees have made it inside a hollow tree-trunk.

So he is clever enough to fly to the nearest man he can find and get him to come and open up the hive for him.

When you are walking in the bush this cheeky bird will come and twitter and flutter just in front of you as you go along, showing

GRATITUDE

you all the time which way to go if you want some honey.

So you follow his lead till at last he brings you to the tree where the honey is stored.

He sits by you while you ply your axe, and in the end you get your honey. Then, if you are a Scout, you will remember to thank the bird who has been so good as to show you where to find it. You do this by leaving a lump of honeycomb for him to eat.

PADDLE YOUR OWN CANOE

The natives here in Kenya say that if you don't do this the bird will appear in front of you again, and just as before lead you with your heart full of hope to another tree, and when you hack it open out will spring a nasty great snake! That's the bird's way of getting a bit of his own back on you. He is a clever bird is the honey-bird!

But it just shows you that, if birds expect you to be grateful for a kindness, how much more other people will expect you to thank them when they try to do you a good turn.

Only you should do this, not from fear of snakes jumping out and getting you by the nose (by the way, you first-aiders, how would you deal with a fellow who had got bitten by a cobra on the top of his proboscis?), but

GRATITUDE

you should return thanks simply because it is the right thing to do.

The Scout Law says "A Scout is courteous".

Every Scout knows the order about camping, that when you break up your camp there are two things which you should leave behind you:

The first is—nothing.

The second—your thanks. Thanks to God for the good time you have had, and thanks to the owner of the land who has let you have the use of it.

COURTESY

As shown by Car-drivers

TALKING about courtesy, I was glad to see the other day that a German visitor to England had written to say that he was agreeably surprised to find that the motor-drivers in our country were generally far more polite to each other than they were in his own or other countries he had visited. Most English drivers now drive their cars with a good-natured spirit of give-and-take for each other, instead of racing and pushing in, and selfishly cutting the other fellow out.

The result of this good feeling is that we have fewer accidents and the work of the traffic police is much lessened.

He quoted as an example the enormous crowd of cars gathered at a meeting at Brook-

COURTESY

lands. He thought there would be an awful mix-up when they all tried to get away at the end of the show, but was astonished to see that all went smoothly, no shouting or cursing or bumping, but everyone taking his turn quietly.

What particularly struck him was the very small number of police present to regulate the traffic. He said that in his country there would have to be fifty where we had only one. He put it down to the courtesy between drivers which largely regulated the traffic.

For a long time cyclists were a danger, not only to motorists but to themselves. They used to take up a lot more of the road than was necessary and expected motor-car drivers to make way for them, and—what was more difficult—to see them in the dark when they

PADDLE YOUR OWN CANOE

only carried a tiny red sparkler on their back mudguard.

Now that is being altered, and in the same way the spirit of comradeship of the road has grown up and they give and take with motorists where they used to be almost at war with one another. British good-nature and courtesy have conquered.

I see that pedestrians have a society to stand up for their rights to use the public roadway any way they like. Even where there is a footpath along the road for them, some of the braver—I won't use a harsher word— prefer to walk on the road . . . and almost always with their backs to the oncoming traffic.

I say "braver" because, though I walk a good deal on the road in the country, I

COURTESY

haven't the pluck or the folly to walk with traffic rushing up behind me. I prefer to go facing the oncoming cars so that I can dodge them if they are not quite under the control of their drivers—which is sometimes the case.

Here again good-natured give-and-take is needed. It just means what I am always saying—don't think only of your own rights and wishes, but see the other fellow's point of view too and help him.

If every boy keeps the fifth Scout Law—A Scout is Courteous—it will soon become the Briton's law, and when everybody is courteous everybody will be safer and happier.

Have a spot of rose, Cousin Hyrie?

GOODWILL

In Rhinos and Elephants

"Hyrie" is a little jungle animal, wild and nervous by nature, but he has been completely tamed by my wife into a very lovable and happy little domestic pet in our house.

The hyrax is, as I have said elsewhere, counted by scientific men to be a relation to

GOODWILL

the elephant and the rhinoceros, although he is no more like a rhino than a Boy Scout is like my boot (except perhaps when he happens to be an ugly enough boy!).

Lately, however, it has happened that even full-grown rhinos have been tamed here in Kenya. But the training has been done by kindness, not by trapping and capturing.

The animals have seen cattle out grazing and have joined them in their enjoyment of good pasture. When the cattle have been quietly herded into their corral at night the rhino has joined in the procession without noticing where he was going. In a day or two he has become accustomed to this routine and has soon discovered that that curious-looking two-legged animal who smells so

PADDLE YOUR OWN CANOE

strange is a thing that brings him nice food in the corral and is a friend and not an enemy. So he soon has no fear and no dislike for him and lets him stroke him and pat him—not that this can give him much pleasure, since, being a rhino, he naturally has a rhinoceros hide, so he could only feel the stroking if it were done with a rake and the patting if done with hammers!

It is much the same with some elephants in Northern Kenya who come into a village there almost every day. They have lost their fear and dislike for men because the people there show no fear or dislike for them. So they are all good friends. Indeed the elephants are very pleased with themselves when the children admire them.

PADDLE YOUR OWN CANOE

It is just the same with people. If you have no fear of the people you meet, and no dislike for them, they will likewise not be afraid or suspicious of you and will be inclined to like you and to be friends.

That is what Scouts find at their International Jamborees when they meet thousands of Scouts of other countries. Being " Brother Scouts " they have no fear of each other and readily become good friends.

Why the " juice " cannot nations do the same?

Sometimes others will like to argue or to quarrel with you, but before you get angry with them try to see the question from their point of view as well as your own and you will probably see that they have some excuse for what they say.

GOODWILL

Your employer, for instance, or foreman, may swear at you for being late or for making some stupid mistake. Well, don't get angry with him, think what you would do if you were in his place and had to correct a fellow who was upsetting his work by being late or careless. You'll understand his reason for being a bit peevish. Always try to see the other fellow's point of view before you argue or quarrel with him, and ninety-nine times out of a hundred you'll end up on friendly terms with him.

Never mind being cursed by your foreman. Cursing is a weakness indulged in by some men who are not strong enough in character to command their temper. Sometimes indeed they are admired for showing their weakness. The Irish writer, Donn Byrne, says—"A horse

PADDLE YOUR OWN CANOE

that don't kick, a man that don't swear, an egg without salt—the back of my hand to all of them."

Scouts have their International Jamboree every four years, at which thousands of them come together from most of the countries of the world. Being "Brother Scouts" they have no fear of each other and they don't dislike a fellow because he happens to be a foreigner or has different habits and customs; they overlook such little differences and enjoy learning about the other chap's ways and doings, and both parties have a jolly time together and make lasting friendships during their stay in camp together.

If boys can do this in all countries whyever can't the men do it too instead of being

GOODWILL

always suspicious or jealous of their neighbours and ready to go to war with them?

I think it would be a good thing if we drowned all the men and let boys rule the world. We should have a cheery world of jolly goodwill and friendliness.

HONOUR

Whacking the Goat

THE Kikuyu tribe had a curious way of making an agreement or treaty, which meant a very bad time for a goat.

The men who were to make the agreement assembled, and a goat with its legs tied was laid down in the middle. Each man carried a stick, and when he had said his say he threw down his stick near the goat.

At the end the presiding chief took up each speaker's stick in turn and repeated very shortly what he had said, and then hit the wretched goat a whack with the stick.

His talk would be something like this:

" Kokobu, whose stick I hold, has complained that Plumface's goats are always grazing on his land "—here he whacked the goat. " Plumface promises that this shall never happen again." Another whack for the goat.

"Semibumpo, whose stick I hold, complains that both Plumface and Kokobu use his stream for watering their goats and then let them stray all over his pasture: but as they promise not to let them wander he agrees to their using his water." Whack. "So, gentlemen, that's that. You have made your promises and will be trusted to carry them out. This dispute is now ended for ever—as dead as this goat."

With that he gives the poor beast a final crack on the head which kills it.

The goat being more or less a sacred animal, none of those present would ever have dared to go back on his promise. It is like a Scout being put on his honour.

I am glad to say, however, that kindness

to animals has now come in and goat-whacking no longer goes on.

But I have sometimes wondered what would have happened if the goat had suddenly jumped up and said—"That's enough of your whacking. I'm fed up with it. It's my turn now, so out you go."

Would the different parties have stuck to their promises? I think not.

The Kikuyu don't know what honour is. They have not a word in their language that

HONOUR

means "honour". And there are several other nations, more civilised than the Kikuyu, who have not yet learned to practise honour. So when they make agreements or treaties they have not even a goat to whack to bind them to carry out their promises, and they cannot be trusted to do so. But a Briton is known all over the world as honourable. "An Englishman's word is as good as his bond" is a saying, meaning that if he says he'll do a thing you can bet your boots he'll do it, just as faithfully as if he'd given a written promise to do it.

When a Spaniard wants to say that he is speaking the exact truth, just as we should say "Really and truly"—or "Scout's honour"—he says "Palabra de inglés" (An Englishman's word).

KEEPING YOUR NERVE
Even when Rhinos Galumph

IN a Belfast tram-car I saw the following notice to passengers: "Spitting is forbidden. Anyone indulging in this habit will render himself liable to the loathing and disgust of his fellow-passengers."

Loathing and disgust of one's fellows is a pretty heavy penalty to pay, but there are sometimes visitors to Kenya who incur it—fellows who go out in motor-cars to shoot big game and lions instead of stalking in a sportsmanlike way.

One man wrote in the Press defending these motor-car heroes, saying that for elderly men or those suffering from dicky hearts motor-cars are essential. I should have thought staying at home would be more essential for them.

KEEPING YOUR NERVE

But there are not many "sportsmen" of this type left now. Fewer people come to Kenya to shoot with the rifle, more come to shoot with the camera, and these are really the best sportsmen because it is far more difficult to stalk sufficiently close to an animal if you want to take his portrait than it is to shoot him with a rifle at some distance away.

The camera man needs to be a particularly clever stalker and also a particularly cool and plucky one. It is nervy work getting close up to a wild and possibly savage animal. Often if the animal gets suspicious it becomes a question of whether to stand or run. Often it is best to stand if you have got the nerve to do so.

Many a man has run when an elephant has

PADDLE YOUR OWN CANOE

come towards him with ears cocked and trunk stretched out. Others who have dared to face such an advance have found that the 'phant was only anxious to see what was there—for he is very shortsighted—and as soon as he found it was a man he sheered off again, anxious to get away from such an unpleasant creature.

But it takes a bit of nerve on the part of the man to stand up to a creature who can be still more unpleasant if he chooses.

That kind of "nerve" can be gained by practice, especially if you have begun as a boy to control yourself.

The soldier excused himself for running away in a battle by saying that his legs got the better of him and ran away with him. Well, you have to control your legs when you

KEEPING YOUR NERVE

are tempted to run away from danger. You have to make yourself face it.

It is the same in a panic when other people are all losing their heads and getting excited, a real MAN will force himself to keep calm and collected. Others seeing him unmoved by the turmoil will probably recover their wits and stand fast.

I was in a theatre once when a lot of people suddenly left their seats and made a rush for the doors. I was in the dress circle and could not see what the trouble was, but a man sitting in front of us jumped up and began yelling "Fire".

As quick as a thought my brother landed a punch behind the man's ear and knocked him down in a heap. People around us had already got up and were anxiously pushing for

PADDLE YOUR OWN CANOE

the doors. There might have been a fatal jam had not an actor rushed on to the stage and shouted "Keep your seats. There is no need for alarm. No fire. Only an elephant, which is to appear in the next act, put his head into the wrong door at the back of the pit."

You see what fatal harm one man might do by not having control of himself, and how one man can save such a situation by keeping cool.

Self-control also means keeping your temper when faced with an angry adversary. The one who keeps cool wins. When two Chinamen quarrel they curse each other and call each other names till one finally loses his temper and hits the other. This means that he has lost the fight because he has come to the end of his flow of insults. The man who keeps himself longest from striking is counted the winner.

Here is a parody of Rudyard Kipling's poem called "If":

> "If you can 'freeze' without a sign of fear
> When crusty rhinos come galumphing near,
> Or face an elephant whose ears and trunk
> Would put most people in an awful funk;
> If you can keep your temper and can laugh
> When bullies rile you with insulting chaff;
> If you can keep our Law through thick and thin
> When others tempt you in the ways of sin;
> If you can stand when men in panic run
> You'll be a Scout, what's more, a MAN, my son."

COURAGE

Of Lions and Lion-hunters

You know the phrase " brave as a lion ", but we never hear " brave as a lion-hunter ". Yet the courage of some of these native hunters is hard to beat.

I told you in the last chapter how, if you are a good stalker *and have the pluck*, you will stand fast when a wild animal comes at you, since it may be only to have a look at you—but also, on the other hand, it may be to charge !

The difficulty is to know when it is which !

So you need also to be a good runner or a good tree-climber, just in case. . . .

A great friend of mine had his own way of overcoming this difficulty. He was a Zulu hunter and we were following up a lion together, tracking him by his spoor.

This led us into a very thick patch of thorny bush, very like a clump of gorsebush in England,  with tunnels under it made by animals using the cover.

My idea was to wait outside and watch for Mr. Lion coming out. But that was not Umpula's idea. His plan, which he carefully explained to me, was for us both to go in and bring the lion out—dead if possible, of course.

PADDLE YOUR OWN CANOE

"Yes, Umpula, that's all very fine, but how?"

"Well, you creep in on all fours with your gun ready, and I will follow close behind you. When you see the lion, shoot, but aim low so that your bullet, even if it misses him, will kick up such a cloud of dust that he will not see us very clearly as he rushes at us. I will then cover both of us with my big shield and as he goes over us I will stab him in the belly with my assegai, and that will be the end of Mr. Lion. Quite simple, you see."

"'M'yes—oh, yes, quite simple." But I was a little doubtful as to whether it wasn't equally simple for the lion, when he found two men wriggling about on their tummies in the bush, to pop on to them and mince them up.

COURAGE

Frankly I didn't like Umpula's idea a bit.

But when you are in a funk you must not on any account show it. Then is the time to whistle and smile as if you liked it. So I put on a sickly grin and dragged myself on hands and knees into the dark hole in the bush.

It certainly heartened me to find that Umpula was following almost on top of me with his shield projecting over my head like a small verandah. This, coupled with the evident keenness and courage of the man, put a small spark of confidence into me, so that presently I found myself going forward with rather a feeling of excitement in the adventure.

On we went, worming our way through the dark tunnel with its many side passages, any one of which might be the lion's retreat. On and on we crawled, my heart in my mouth

PADDLE YOUR OWN CANOE

all the time, till presently there was a dull gleam of light ahead and soon we saw the end of the tunnel leading into the open. "All clear" sounded joyously in my ears while my tongue was proclaiming to Umpula "What a pity, he has sneaked away."

But that man had no sense of fear in him. Some people are born that way—most of us

COURAGE

are not. But the bravest of all are those who, while feeling funky, are so strong-minded that they conquer their fear and don't allow it to show itself to others. By doing this you can inspire courage in those around you who may not be feeling too happy themselves.

Here in Kenya young men of the Masai tribe, as of others, are taught to be courageous even at the risk of their lives. I wish we had such a school for Scouts—though I am bound to say that hundreds of them have shown that they have that bravery without needing a school to teach them.

The school for the Masai is, in fact, a lion hunt. A whole party go out, each armed with only one assegai and a shield. When a lion is found the hunters form a wide circle round him and gradually close in on him. The lion tries in various directions to get away but everywhere finds his passage barred by men advancing towards him.

The circle draws closer and closer, till the warriors are almost shoulder to shoulder. At last the lion sees that his only chance is to charge and break through the ring. He dashes at the nearest man and possibly crashes him down with his weight and gashes one or two others with his claws, but others drive their spears into him with fatal effect.

The man who first spears the lion is given his mane to wear as a distinguishing head-dress. This is looked on as such a high honour—like the Bronze Cross of the Scouts—that every man is eager to be the first to tackle the animal. Consequently, before the

COURAGE

lion can charge he is generally charged by men anxious to get their spear into him regardless of the chance that they will be killed or terribly mauled in the attempt.

Some school, that!

KEEPING YOUR PECKER UP

Bravery against Odds

A WILD boar came to the edge of the jungle and looked out across the plain. His wife and kiddies had come in in a great hurry saying there was a horrid beast of a man out there riding on a horse and he had frightened them out of their lives.

Father Boar looked out and there he saw, half a mile away, the man riding along looking very uppish and insolent.

So he said to himself—"I don't care whether that fellow is carrying one of those noise-making tubes which kills or a spear which wounds, I'm going to larn him not to frighten women and children."

So off he trotted in the direction of the unsuspecting horseman.

KEEPING YOUR PECKER UP

Mind you, I saw this with my own eyes.

In a short while he increased his pace to a lolloping canter, with his ears pricked and a nasty look in his eye.

Then, when he got within a hundred yards of the rider, he suddenly changed his pace into a rushing gallop and charged full split at his foe, utterly regardless of any danger that it might mean for himself. A few moments later, coupled with his gruff roaring grunt, there was a crash as he hurled his weight upward from underneath the horse, and a wild yell from the man as he and his mount were capsized head over heels in the air and banged in a heap on the ground.

The old boar looked at them for a moment and then turned and trotted quietly back to his lair, wagging his old head from side to

side as he went and plainly saying to himself—
"That'll larn 'em!" Grand old warrior! He might easily have remained hidden in the jungle when the enemy came in sight, but with his chivalrous desire to protect women and children he went forward bravely to face danger, although it might mean death for himself.

That was a lesson to us in courage and self-sacrifice.

KEEPING YOUR PECKER UP

I could tell you dozens of instances like this one of the courage of wild animals of many kinds.

If animals show courage how much more is it up to every man to show it.

There are so many ways in which a boy can develop his courage. I am glad to feel that in the Scouts many hundreds of boys have won the Bronze Cross for heroism and the Silver Cross for life-saving with risk to personal safety.

Then there is another kind of courage for which we have the bronze letter C. badge, the Cornwell Badge, for courage in enduring pain. It is named after Boy Cornwell of the Royal Navy who at the Battle of Jutland in the Great War stuck to his post although severely wounded. He afterwards died of his wound.

But though he might have gone away to the dressing-station he thought it was his duty to endure the pain and stick  to his gun rather than think of himself. That was the true courage of a real Scout.

But courage is needed too for much more ordinary conditions. Suppose you are working in a factory or office, day after day, at work which doesn't interest you; it needs courage to stick to it. Don't think only of your own feelings but remember that your work, even if it is drudgery to you, is helping your firm to

KEEPING YOUR PECKER UP

go ahead; it is producing something of value to other people, possibly to the nation, and also it brings in money to you which helps you to help your family. So take courage and " stick to it ".

I can't here go into the hundreds of forms of courage which can be practised by a man, but the highest example we have is that of Christ. He knew that if He carried on His work of saving souls He would be cruelly crucified alive, but He never flinched. He put His Duty first and Himself second and with sublime courage faced His sacrifice for the good of others.

HUMOUR

A Lesson from Algernon

WHEN I was young and respectable—which is a great many years ago—I was fond of acting plays.

In one play called "Whitebait at Greenwich" I acted the part of a waiter at an hotel: he had been deserted by his parents, but he had in his pocket a police handbill giving a description of his father which, as I remember it, said:

"Deserted his child, a man surname unknown, Christian name Benjamin: had on when last seen fustian jacket and corduroy breeches. Height 5 ft. 10 in. in his shoes", etc.

So whenever a man came into the hotel I enquired whether his name happened to be Benjamin and when it wasn't I was fairly

HUMOUR

disappointed. At last a couple arrived and I heard her call him Benjamin. I got out my tape-measure and in pretending to dust him down I secretly and eagerly took his measure —5 ft. 8 in. In a fury of excitement I jerked up his foot to measure the thickness of his boot. In spite of his indignation and struggles I found it two inches thick. I immediately claimed him affectionately as my father and her as my mother. Their indignation was great, as they were only cousins and not married, and of course had no knowledge of me.

Well—often as I acted this part I never could help shaking with inward laughter at the absurdity and humour of the situation, when I ought to have been thinking only of doing my bit.

PADDLE YOUR OWN CANOE

I once had, in India, a young wild boar as a pet. He wasn't much of a pet really because he was so very wild. He lived in the compound which was a mixture of garden and paddock, and this he shared with my horses. One of these, a fine English mare, was a grand hunter. In India our hunting took the form of hunting wild pig, and the mare entered into it with such zest that she would follow a boar almost without guidance from the rider, and when she overtook him she would strike at the pig with her forefeet.

Well, when she saw Master Algernon—that was my little boar's name—in the compound she made a rush at him, but he dodged her and scooted into the bushes. After that escapade the little villain used to watch the

mare from his hiding-place, and when she was quietly grazing he would creep out and stalk her from behind and then suddenly startle her with the gruff snarl of a grown-up boar. She would jump out of her skin, almost, with alarm, and then, seeing who it was, would go for him for all she was worth. But he was a deal quicker than she and just when she thought she was going to bash him with her

PADDLE YOUR OWN CANOE

hoof he would jump aside and be off in another direction before she could turn. This was repeated over and over again till both paused for breath and to rest.

This game went on day after day, Algernon thoroughly enjoying himself, the mare angrily getting well exercised. It was really a dangerous game for Algernon, but he had the sense of humour to see the fun in what was otherwise a risky adventure.

That sense of humour, of being able to see a funny side to even a dangerous or unpleasant situation, is of the highest value to a man in going through life.

Some people have not got that sense and when misfortune hits them or things look black for them they have not got a ray of sunshine to lighten their gloom, but a fellow

HUMOUR

who has accustomed himself to see a funny side in everything can go through the difficulties and dangers with a light heart and, what is more, can give hope and confidence to others around him.

DON'T SWANK

Or you may have to live in a rabbit-hole

I HAVE told you how the ostriches strutted about looking very proud of themselves and very superior to all other birds. But, as Mrs. Oryx said, they only succeeded in looking silly. And that was exactly what other birds thought of them. Therefore, when the chief ostrich gave out that he was going to be king of the

DON'T SWANK

birds, the birds said that nobody could make himself their king. The king would have to be elected and they agreed that whichever bird could fly the highest should be king.

So they started flying matches, and the ostrich, who had hoped to be king, couldn't fly higher than he could hop—and that wasn't far. So our ugly friend Mr. Vulture soared up into the sky, feeling sure that nobody could go higher than himself—and up he went, high above skylarks and other high-flyers.

And when he could see no more birds above him he cried, "Hooray! I've flown highest."

"Not a bit of it"—cried the small voice of a little African bird called the "Ting-Ticky".

Ting-ticky, unknown to the vulture, had hung on to a feather under his wing when he started and so was carried up by him when he soared. Now when the vulture had reached the top of his flight Ting-Ticky came out and flew up above him saying "I'm King of the Birds". "No, you're not," shouted the vulture as he soared up a bit higher, not knowing that Ting-Ticky had settled on his back as he did so. So when he had got very high he stopped soaring: but out came Ting-Ticky again, flew up a foot or two above him, and squeaked—" I'm King of the Birds ".

This went on two or three times till the vulture got so tired that he could soar no more, and he gave in.

So Ting-Ticky proclaimed that he had

DON'T SWANK

made the record for high flying and must be made "King of the Birds".

But the vulture was so angry with him that he resolved to kill him. Ting-Ticky heard of this and promptly made his palace down a rabbit-hole.

Well, you can't do much king-ing from a rabbit-hole. Ting-Ticky soon found that his boasting about having won the high-flying record did not have much effect on the other birds, because they knew that he had not flown up under his own power but had gone up like that aeroplane the "Mercury" which sits on the back of another plane to be lifted up into the air. So they laughed at his boasting and when he tried squeaking out orders to them from the safety of his rabbit-hole they only jeered at him.

PADDLE YOUR OWN CANOE

So as a king he was a failure.

I have known several Ting-Tickies among boys—not among Scouts OF COURSE: boys who boasted or talked a lot about what they could do at cricket or running or swimming. They were top-dogs according to their own account. That was all right till somebody put them to the test and showed them up as humbugs. They would then have been glad of a rabbit-hole as a refuge from the laughter and chaff of the fellows they had tried to take in.

Never buck about your wonderful powers. If you have them there is no need to tell about them, other fellows will see them fast enough for themselves.

ON "STICKING IT OUT"

In a Drain-Pipe

I HAVE just heard a new version of the old game of "Are you there?"

It happened to a cyclist here in Africa who was biking down a steep hill at full speed. The road took a sharp turn at the bottom and as he rounded the corner he found the way blocked by a huge elephant standing broadside on to the traffic. He was going too fast to stop, but he slewed his machine sharply round the elephant's hindquarters where there was just room for him to get by, steadying himself with his hand against the animal's hind legs as he did so.

It was a close shave, and he drew a deep breath of relief as he ran clear. But his relief didn't last long. It was just as if a small urchin had pinched a traffic police constable behind. In a moment the elephant had swung round, evidently saying—" Here, you. What are you playing at? Come here. D'you hear?"

But the cyclist didn't stop. He put on his best speed to get away. Then he saw, to his horror, that the road, after crossing a culvert, went up a steep hill. Looking back he saw that the elephant was coming along full split after him, and there was no hope of his being able to get up that hill before the animal would have him out of the saddle and trampled to death underfoot.

He thought and acted quickly. He had to. It was just a matter of seconds whether he was to go on living or end up a mangled mess.

ON "STICKING IT OUT"

He ran his bike into the ditch and as he did so he dived off it himself and slithered into the culvert under the road. This would have been all right if the elephant had not seen him do it, but that's just what the old 'phant HAD done. And then began the game of "Are you there?"

ARE YOU THERE?
NB The culvert, with its contents, is supposed to be underneath the Road.

PADDLE YOUR OWN CANOE

The elephant knelt down at one end of the culvert and sent his long trunk investigating, evidently asking the question. But Mr. Cyclist crept as far away from it as he could, and lay low and said nothing.

Presently the trunk was withdrawn, and for the second time the cyclist's sigh of relief was cut short when he found the trunk snaking in from the opposite end of the culvert and he had just time to scramble away to the other end.

And so the game went on endlessly backwards and forwards, "Are you there?" repeated again and again from either end.

The game proved so popular—with the elephant—that it might have gone on till now. But it was tiring work and at last the elephant went off to get a drink of water. When he

ON "STICKING IT OUT"

came back and went on with the game it was some time before he noticed that the bicycle was no longer in the ditch, nor was the cyclist still playing the game in the culvert.

HOW TO BE FIT

LESSONS FROM MEN AND BEASTS

The Kikuyu Dance

I HAVE just seen what I have long wanted to see, namely, a dance by young men of the Kikuyu tribe in their gala dress.

I told you some time ago how the boys of this tribe have to go through a pretty stiff examination to see whether they are fit to be promoted to be men in the tribe.

Only a few years ago—well, in 1896-1900 to be exact—before the British settled the country and gave their protection to the Kikuyu, these people had to fight against the neighbouring tribes, the Masai and the Nandis, who were warriors and lived by raiding the others.

So, though the Kikuyu were good at growing crops of food, they had to train them-

HOW TO BE FIT

selves to be strong and active and so to be able to protect their homes and their crops against raiders.

It was rather like what we are going through in Britain to-day, when neighbouring countries are warlike and threaten to raid our more peaceful and prosperous lands. We too have to train ourselves and carry out the Scouts' motto "Be Prepared" to protect ourselves.

Although the Kikuyu don't need to prepare for fighting now that they are protected by us, they still keep up the dances and other practices which make their boys into healthy, strong and active men, useful in peace-time for making their country prosperous.

Just in the same way, Scouts make themselves strong and active and healthy so as to

PADDLE YOUR OWN CANOE

Be Prepared when they are men to be able to do good work towards making their country successful and prosperous.

The Kikuyu don't possess gymnasiums and drill-instructors, but make themselves fit with lots of outdoor exercise and dancing—and simple feeding.

In the same way Scouts don't depend on gymnasiums and drill-sergeants but get their health and strength through active games, hiking and camping, Morris-dancing, climbing, swimming, etc.

A boy told me that he wanted to be a strong muscular fellow, but being only an errand-boy he could not get much chance of attending drill. I told him that drill is not necessary. As an errand-boy he had the best possible chance of making himself strong and

HOW TO BE FIT

healthy, because his work took him a great deal into the open air and gave him a certain amount of exercise. Those are the two important things for making a chap strong, air and exercise. But when out walking don't just slope along all anyhow: brace yourself up, swell your ribs and your chest as you walk, and stiffen the muscles of your legs.

Play active games like football, running, jumping, swimming and hiking, and especially climbing. With this kind of exercise your muscles very soon grow, provided that you keep it up steadily. Before long you will find your body filling out and you get that jolly feeling of never

being tired but of being ready for any tough job at any time.

There is another way of looking at it too. Remember that God has, as it were, lent you your body for your lifetime, and it is up to you to make the best use of it. Make it as perfect a body as you can by giving yourself plenty of air, exercise, good food and cleanliness. Think of that as part of your duty to God and carry it out in your everyday life. In that way you will be Healthy and Happy yourself and will also be strong enough to be Helpful to other people.

For the ceremony of passing their tests for manhood, one of which is this dance, the Kikuyu boys paint their faces white and their legs with white stripes. They wear a white shirt, belted at the waist, and a fur neck

collar of black and white colobus monkey skins. Each dancer carries a fly-whisk made of giraffe's tail in the right hand, and a stick in the left. He also wears a little bell strapped to his knee. The two leaders carry small wooden shields on their left arms with a small iron bead attached to the shield by a thong which they rattle.

The Kikuyu, unlike other native tribes, have no musical instruments and no drums; they supply their own music by singing and they dance by bouncing with both feet together and they keep up the dance for hour after hour as a test of their endurance.

I wonder for how many hours you could keep up Morris-dancing!

What Hyrie can teach

You may remember why it is that the hyrax is like you—an animal without a tail. I told

"HYRIE"

STERN VIEW
Stalking an Intruder

you in a former book how the hyraxes were chosen by the Creator to fit all the other animals with their tails, because they were the most active, plucky, and trustworthy animals in the jungle. They did this difficult job rapidly and without making a mistake. It would have been awful if, for instance, they had fitted a pig's tail on to a horse or a peacock's tail on to a cat; but they didn't. They fitted every one correctly, and then to their horror they found that there were no tails left over for themselves—and so they have to go without.

PADDLE YOUR OWN CANOE

But they don't seem to mind much. At any rate our tame little "Hyrie" is as cheerful and bright as an animal could be. When we have our early tea in the morning he is always there and eager for it. He clambers up on to my wife's shoulder and after licking her ear he whines until she lifts up a saucer of tea (with milk and sugar) to him and he gollops it down eagerly. Then he jumps on to me for his breakfast of carrot-tops, rose-leaves, and bits of biscuit. After this he goes mad and does his physical exercises. He tears round the room a few times, clambers up and down the backs of chairs and twiddles himself into all sorts of contortions in doing so, exercising every part of his body. Then he'll clamber at a run up a chair and from the top of the back of it

HOW TO BE FIT

will take a flying leap on to the mantelpiece, rush along it, another flying leap on to the window-sill, climb up the edge of the casement window to the very top, and thence drop plump on to the floor. All done at tremendous speed with never a mistake, thoroughly enjoying himself.

For a change he will suddenly rush at me and seize my coat in his teeth, shake it, and be out of sight under the bed the next second. If I catch him he rolls on his back and wriggles and mouths me while I tickle him, loving a good rough and tumble.

Yes, he is tremendously active and, from continual practice, is wonderfully strong for so small an animal. (He is only the size of a small rabbit and much like one except that he has short ears and no tail.)

PADDLE YOUR OWN CANOE

Of course he can climb trees, that is his job and chief delight, and he will spring from branch to branch with amazing rapidity and accuracy—never missing his grip.

Sometimes the big Blue Birds attack him, but he is not afraid of them. He will dart away from them or will sit tight and in his turn will run at them when they settle—not a bit afraid of their beaks. I don't know now whether they are really attacking him or, as I believe, they are merely having a game with him.

It is laughable to see him climb up the tall polished legs of my tripod telescope; directly he gets to the top he curls himself round a leg and slides plump to the ground; up he goes and does it all over again, and when he has had enough he continues his upward

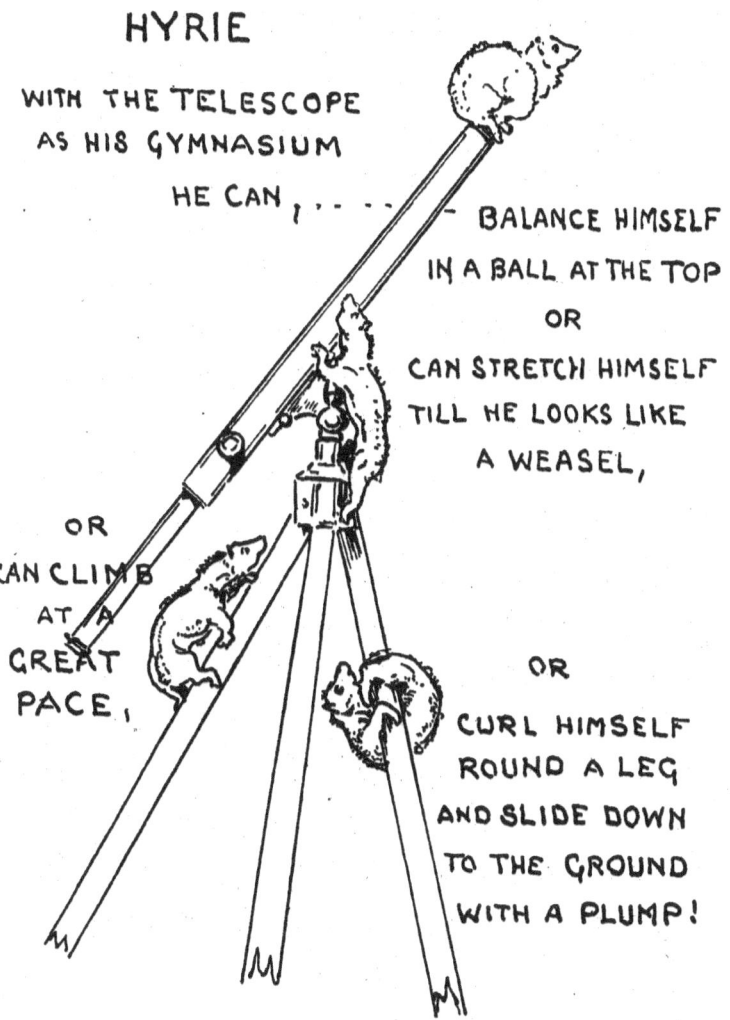

climb on the polished brass of the upright telescope till he gets to the top and squats there on the object-glass looking around for something else to climb. He always wants to climb yet higher, so we call him "Highery" instead of "Hyrie". And that's a good hint for you, always to want to improve, to go one better than before in whatever you do.

Well, if a little animal like that can make himself so strong and active and fearless and healthy, simply through practising for himself, surely every boy could do the same if he set himself to do it. Why should you need a drill-sergeant to teach you to "bend and stretch" or a high-class indoor gymnasium to teach you to develop your muscles?

You can do not only as well but a jolly sight better in God's open-air by running and

HOW TO BE FIT

jumping, climbing trees or ropes or rocks. Swimming is another most excellent way of strengthening your limbs, while it gives you pluck and confidence.

Hyrie can teach you a thing or two about proper feeding too. He will eagerly eat many kinds of leaves and fruit, but others he won't touch because he knows they're not good for him. What boy has the strength of mind to do that?

If you have that sense you'll grow strong and healthy, my son.

Then, too, Hyrie is so jolly cheery and friendly, loves his human playfellows and does all his exercises as a bit of fun with them; so follow his example, enjoy your exercises and turn them into laughing games with your pals, and you'll be a happier man, my son.

PADDLE YOUR OWN CANOE

How to Jump Six Feet

I HAVE to-day had a talk with a man who has been visiting a native tribe in the Belgian Congo territory, north-west of Kenya. These people are called the Watussi and are very superior to most of the tribes about them.

For one thing the men are very tall, generally well over six feet, sometimes up to seven feet. Also they are amazingly active and strong.

One thing they are specially good at is jumping, and when I was told that they could jump their own height I did not believe it.

But my friend then showed me a photograph (which I have copied here) of Mr. Patrick Balfour, who, with his hat on, measures over six feet, being jumped by one of the

Watussi. Mr. Balfour in his book "The Lords of the Equator" describes these people and says that he couldn't help feeling a bit anxious when he saw the men running straight at him, and it was hard not to flinch; but one after another they sprang at him, tucked up their legs and cleared him all right—as in the picture. Then he tells the secret of their wonderful activity and strength; they get it by training themselves in their boyhood.

The boys of the tribe are all keen on making themselves athletic and, like the Kikuyu, they go in a lot for dancing all kinds of active dances, full of jumping, twisting their bodies, stamping and rushing madly, but all in strict time. This they keep up for tremendously long periods till they get into good hard condition. And—note this, Scouts—all through the performance the boys keep smiling!

Don't forget that when you are doing your exercises. When they are not dancing, the Watussi practise throwing the javelin, high jumping, and running. In this way they make themselves healthy and strong; they don't need a gymnasium or a drill-instructor to teach them—they just do it for themselves.

In some countries abroad the boys are forced to go through a lot of drill and physical training by instructors in order to make them strong. This is necessary because they don't play active games and only slop about doing nothing to make themselves fit.

Luckily British boys are not like that. They are keen on playing football and other athletic games and take up Scouting with all its outdoor activities like hiking and climbing, swimming, folk-dancing, and wide games. In this way they, like the Watussi, are making themselves into healthy, active and manly fellows—but I haven't heard of any of you jumping six feet as yet! Perhaps it will come—eh?

THE DUTY OF SERVICE
AND HOW TO BE PREPARED

Scouts on His Majesty's Service

TALKING of whistling when there's trouble, I remember in the Great War bombs had fallen on Liverpool Street Station, London, and had killed a number of people among the crowd there. The enemy aeroplanes had passed on and the crowd, like a good English one, were calmly going about getting their tickets and entering their trains, when suddenly there was a cry that the bombers were returning.

This started a rush for the underground passage leading to the tube railway, and there was danger of a panic and a fatal crush. But a voice called out "They won't be back for twenty minutes", and above all the shuffle and noise of the crowd someone whistled

THE DUTY OF SERVICE

"Wait till the clouds roll by!" This raised a laugh and the chorus was started and in a few minutes everybody was calm and comforted. There was no more rushing; people went quietly down into the safe refuge of the Underground.

Well, that offers a hint to you Scouts who have volunteered to do National Service if war should break out again.

Any boy can whistle a tune. If he can keep his head when others are getting panicky, and can then have the cheek to whistle that tune at the top of his whistle, he may do a very great service to the hundreds of people around him by setting them an example of cool cheerfulness when things are looking bad.

What a triumph it would be for one small boy to save a crowd from disaster! One boy's whistle can be like the traffic policeman's white gauntlet and stop the rush of a whole crowd. "Be Prepared" to do it when the time comes.

Being Prepared

The Scouts have been putting on a tremendous lot of good dramatic shows lately; "Gang Shows", Pantomimes, Rally Displays, and so on.

It is wonderful when you come to think of what a lot of rehearsal these big shows take if they are to be a success. And in this case it is all the more wonderful because, just at the time when important rehearsals were on, the alarm of war was sounded and the Scouts had to take up their many duties for the

public services. They have almost had to do their rehearsals in gas-masks!

It reminds me of a time, long ago, when my Regiment was in Afghanistan and we were rehearsing the play "The Pirates of Penzance". We had no room in which to rehearse, so it had to be out of doors. But there was always the danger of fanatical tribesmen rushing down on us at any moment with their nasty great knives, awfully unpleasant things. So each performer brought his sword with him to rehearsal, and these weapons we stuck up in the ground to mark the boundaries of our stage, and they were at the same time handy in case of an attack.

Talking of rehearsals, I want you to understand how necessary it is to have plenty of preparation if your show, of whatever kind, is to be a success.

If you are going to run a race you know how important it is to get well trained for it first. It is no use to go and box a fellow if you haven't first learned and practised boxing. What a lovely pair of black eyes you would get if you hadn't!

Once I had a swimming exercise for my

THE DUTY OF SERVICE

men and horses. Of course only men who could swim should have attended this parade. To our horror and excitement one man was very nearly drowned. When we had pumped him out and artificially respirated him, we asked him whether he had learned to swim. He said "No", but as everybody else seemed able to swim he had supposed that he could too, so he went in with the rest and found that he couldn't!

If you want to get on in life, you have to be able to read and write, and you can't do that unless you go to school first and learn how. In the same way, if you want to be a manly fellow and to be prepared to help other people and to save life, or to do public service, you learn and practise it first by being a Boy Scout.

A Government 'Authority' picking out a boy for duty.

I am very glad to hear that everywhere Scouts are preparing themselves to be useful if they should be called out for service. The thing is to find out from your Scoutmaster what sort of duty you will be wanted to do, and then practise yourself for it so that you will be able to do it really well when called upon.

Signalling is one thing that will be a valuable bit of service if you can do it really

THE DUTY OF SERVICE

well. It is no use at all if you are likely to bungle a message, so practise it hard.

Cyclist messengers will be needed, not only able to ride a bike and repair it but able to find their way from place to place by day or night (night requires practice) and to carry a message in the head word for word correctly and to deliver it clearly.

Practise your first-aid knowledge; one is so apt to forget small details unless one practises them often.

After all the best way to qualify for service is to be able to show on your arm the First Class badge or better still that of a King's Scout.

So I say to you all—go on, work away at your First Aid, signalling, boatmanship, A.R.P., airplane, street traffic, coast watching, conducting children, fire, messenger and other duties. Prepare yourselves for one or other of these duties. Have lots of rehearsal in peace-time, while you have not to be hampered by gas-masks or swords, and so be ready at a moment's notice to take up your duties in service for your country when the call comes. Everybody knows now how useful Scouts can be.

So Be Prepared if an emergency comes, for, as in Nelson's time, England will expect that every man that day will do his duty.

Duty. Yes, that's the thing. Efficiency is all very well, but inside there must be something more, there must be courage and pluck and the determination to do your duty no matter what risk or danger it means to yourself.

ELEPHANTS EARNING THE VICTORIA CROSS

HELPFULNESS

Taught by an Elephant

A GREAT elephant hunter who died last week once described how he shot at and wounded a big bull elephant. The rest of the herd, alarmed by the shot, took to their heels, leaving the wounded one staggering about in a dazed condition. Another shot only wounded him again without killing him, but the sound of it hastened the rest of the herd in their flight—all except two. These two bulls were angered by it and stopped to look back. Seeing their comrade swaying in his tracks and unable to get up a bank to follow them, they bravely faced the dreaded rifle fire and went back to help him. They placed themselves one on each side of him and pressing their heavy bodies against him they almost lifted him as they slowly supported him away from danger.

If they had been soldiers rescuing a comrade at risk to their own lives on the battlefield they would have been awarded the Victoria Cross. They were only wild beasts, yet they showed us an example of true helpfulness to a comrade in distress, even if they had to face risks to carry it out.

HELPFULNESS

Some of us are sometimes not inclined to lend a hand to other people, even when there are no risks, because it means giving up some time and some little pleasure.

What do you think of this, chaps? One day last year a little wizened old bloke cycled up to the office of the Department of Labour in Washington and asked to see the Commissioner at the head of it. He said he wanted to save a Russian who was ordered to be sent back from America to Russia, and who did not want to go as he would be shot if he got back there.

The Commissioner said "Sorry: it can't be done. He comes from Russia and he must go back to Russia."

So the little old bloke got on to his bike and cycled to the White House, President

Roosevelt's residence. There he persisted in saying that he must see the President himself, no one else would do.

Finally the President agreed to see him and heard his tale. The President asked him about himself and learned that he was a Jew and had borrowed money and the bike to enable him to come all the way from Texas to appeal for the Russian.

So the President said "Then I suppose this Russian is a Jew and that's why you're interested in him. You Jews do stick to each other."

"Oh no," replied the little man. "He is not a Jew, he is a Greek Church Catholic."

"Then why do you want to help him?"

"I don't see that a man's religion matters.

HELPFULNESS

He is a fellow creature in distress and that's enough to make me want to help him."

The President sent out an order that the Russian was not to be deported and that Mr. Cohen would take charge of him and get him employment.

Well, that Mr. Cohen was well-known to everybody in his home town, Galveston, as a man who spent his life in doing good turns to others. If his body was small his heart was the biggest in the city. He went about doing good, it was his hobby. Directly he heard of anyone wanting help he jotted down the name and address on his shirt-cuff.

Every day his cuff had its list and he trotted about the city, visiting each of the distressed, doing what he could for each of them although he was a poor man himself.

PADDLE YOUR OWN CANOE

He crossed off each name on the cuff when he had paid his visit and did not go home at night till all on his cuff that day had been crossed off. He once said "Many men get exercise and fun by playing golf. I get mine by going about helping people."

That is just what the Boy Scouts are doing when they carry out the Scout's Promise "to help other people *at all times*"—that is to say at all times, whether convenient to themselves or not; nor do they care what creed, or class, or country the other belongs to. They don't have shirt-cuffs as a rule on which to write down the cases they want to deal with, they keep their shirt-sleeves rolled up ready to take on any job. But they wear a neckerchief and in this they tie knots to

HELPFULNESS

remind them of the good turns they have to do.

But as to that Mr. Cohen, I take off my hat to him and would like to shake his hand. Wouldn't you?

RESPONSIBILITY

Learned in a Scout Patrol

I HAD a very nice letter this week from a Scout in France in which he said he had read my life and wanted to make his life like mine, and he hoped that in the end he would also be a General.

So I told him to let me know when he reached that rank; but in the meantime being a General is not all beer and skittles, nor is it all wearing fine uniform and decorations; it also means an awful responsibility in war. Few people seem to think of that, but it is a terrible thing for any man to feel that hundreds of lives depend on his word of command; and that is what a General has to face.

It is bad enough for a judge when he puts

RESPONSIBILITY

on the black cap and sentences a murderer to death to satisfy the law; but it is far worse for a General when he has to decide to send a great number of fine young soldiers to be slaughtered or maimed in order to win a battle.

After the Great War quite a number of our Generals died, although they were not very old, from heart-failure. In my own mind I feel sure that this was largely because of the strain which was put on the heart through this big responsibility.

The pilot of an air-liner is trusted by all his passengers to bring them safely through the risks of the flight.

A captain of a ship also has a big responsibility upon him, since the lives of all on board depend on him in peace or in war.

PADDLE YOUR OWN CANOE

But our naval officers are known all over the world for their fearlessness and self-reliance.

How do they get this? It is because they are trained from boyhood to take on any job and to carry it through on their own—they are taught to accept responsibility.

I remember the time when the sailors in the Royal Navy were older men than now, strong hefty seamen wearing beards. But the officers began their career quite young. A midshipman in those days was only a boy of fourteen or fifteen, but he was given a responsible job; he was put in regular charge of a boat and her crew. There one saw a little whipper-snapper of fifteen commanding men of twice his age. And they obeyed his orders without question. That was *discipline*.

In the siege of Mafeking I found that

boys, although they were only boys, could be trusted to carry out duties which were ordinarily done by men. The boys there were given the responsibility for taking messages from one part of the defences to another even when in danger of their lives under fire.

So, in the Scout movement, we give responsibility to boys by putting them in charge of patrols of six or eight other boys. The Patrol Leader is responsible for the efficiency and smartness of his Patrol. The

Scouts in his Patrol obey his orders, not from fear of punishment, as in naval or military discipline, but because they are a team playing together and backing up their leader for the honour and success of the Patrol.

And the Patrol Leader, in training and leading his Patrol, is gaining practice and experience for being a fellow who can take responsibility, just as the midshipman through commanding his boat's crew is learning to become an officer in command of a battleship.

Also, besides training his Patrol, the Patrol Leader has to *lead* it, that is, he must be at least as good as any of his Scouts at the different jobs they have to do; he must never ask a fellow to do anything he would not do himself, and he must never have a " down " on anyone but get their enthusiasm

RESPONSIBILITY

and willing work by cheerily encouraging their efforts.

In every line of life young men are wanted who can be trusted to take responsibility and leadership—in the Services, in business, in industry, everywhere. So the Patrol Leader who has made a success with his Patrol has every chance of making a success of his life when he goes out into the world.

SELF-SACRIFICE

Heroes of the Antarctic

EVERY Scout knows the story of the death of Captain Oates who gave his life to save others on Captain Scott's expedition to the South Pole; but the full story of his life has only lately been told by Commander Bernacchi, O.B.E. He calls the book "A Very Gallant Gentleman".

For that is how Oates was described on the cross which Surgeon Atkinson afterwards put up to his memory near to the spot where he died.

Oates had been very delicate as a boy and it will be encouraging to any weakly lad to know that he grew up to be an exceptionally strong and plucky young man. He was an officer in the Inniskilling Dragoons, which

SELF-SACRIFICE

now forms part of my old Regiment, the 5th Dragoon Guards (now known as the 5th Royal Inniskilling Dragoon Guards).

He was tremendously popular in the Regiment because he was a very keen soldier, a very good sportsman, and he loved his men and his horses.

He was well off and so was able to afford to run a pack of hounds for the Regiment and to play polo and sail a yacht. There was no need for him to work, but he showed later that he could turn his hand to any kind of job, no matter how hard.

In the Boer War, although he had only just joined the Service, he quickly distinguished himself by his courage and self-sacrifice. He had command of a patrol of half a dozen men when they encountered a force of Boers who opened fire on them. Two of their horses were shot and several men slightly wounded. Twice the Boers asked him to surrender, but each time he returned the same answer—"We came to fight, not to surrender." He saw that it was hopeless to fight the numbers against him, so he told his men to slip away one by one while he remained firing at the enemy to cover their retreat. When they got safely away and it came to his turn to go, a shot smashed his leg. The Boers cleared off, but he lay the whole day long in agony till night came and a search party found him and brought him in.

Ten years later, in 1910, when he heard of Captain Scott's plans for going to the South Pole, he volunteered and was accepted.

SELF-SACRIFICE

Of Captain Scott, Commander Bernacchi tells us that, nine years before this, he had commanded the National Antarctic Expedition in the "Discovery" (now the headquarters of the Sea Scouts). This expedition had returned after three years with the richest results, geographical and scientific, ever brought from high southern latitudes. King Edward VII Land had been discovered and the Great Ice Barrier had been surveyed. The "Discovery" had remained frozen up for two years at the foot of Mount Erebus. Most valuable scientific results had been obtained.

A sledge journey to the far South with Dr. Wilson and Lieut. Shackleton had been made to the mountains and to the plains which led to the South Pole.

PADDLE YOUR OWN CANOE

Arctic explorers had hitherto all been naval men or scientists. Oates was the first soldier to be accepted for such work, and right well he upheld the name of the Army. But he took a very humble position in the expedition; he had to go in charge of twenty ponies which were to drag the sledges of the party.

He became their groom and stableman, a difficult job in a crowded ship, with wild bad-tempered ponies in stormy seas. When they got ashore on the ice of the Antarctic, he had to train them to pull sledges. One pony was his special favourite—a perfect little devil named "Christopher". Christopher wanted to eat anybody who came near him, and if he couldn't reach you with his teeth he would try to land a kick on you with his heels. He would not allow harness to be put

SELF-SACRIFICE

on him and so had to be thrown down before that could be done. But once he was harnessed he pulled his sledge like a good 'un.

When the expedition landed from the ship on the 17th February 1911 and built their hut, it was distant about 900 miles from the South Pole. Farther along the coast, about 400 miles from them, another expedition of Norwegians under Amundsen had landed about the same time, meaning also to be the first to reach the Pole. So, though neither party knew what the other was doing, it became a sort of race between them. Scott's party sent out food supplies on sledges to be dumped at different points along their route, but it was desperately difficult work amid the snow and ice and blizzards.

At last, when the long dark night of

winter was over, the expedition moved southward, some twelve men with sledges loaded with food and tents.

Their journey lay at first over some 400 miles of permanent ice covered with snow, then a climb up a mountain range over a glacier 160 miles long and rising to over 9,000 feet above the sea. Once this was passed, they were on the high plains for another 300 miles.

But the difficulties were enormous. Terrific winds and snowstorms had to be faced, while underfoot the snow was often soft and deep, with holes and crevasses into which the men or the ponies and dogs were in danger of falling, while the ice over which they travelled was, in some places, a mass of waves and cliffs and pinnacles, in which they had to

SELF-SACRIFICE

wander for miles before they could find a way through. It was not long before the ponies got exhausted and died, or had to be shot to feed the dogs, and the dogs themselves followed suit, so that in the end the men had to do the dragging of the sledges.

When they had established depots of food at different points, eight of the party were sent back and the four strongest were picked out by Scott to go with him to do the final rush to the Pole. These were Wilson, Evans, Oates, and Bowers.

They started off on the 17th November. It was a long struggle for them, but buoyed up with the hope of winning the race and constantly encouraged by the untiring energy and hopefulness of their leader, they pushed on and on, day after day, and week after week,.

across these never-ending snow plains. At long last, on 17th January, 1912, they sighted a flag and their hearts sank as they came on the tracks of men and dogs and sleighs.

Amundsen had reached the place before them!

Thus they had got to their destination, the South Pole, but it was a bitter disappointment to find that they were not the first to do it. Then they turned to tackle the long journey back to their base, no longer buoyed up with the hope of being the first to gain the Pole, but depressed with the knowledge that they had lost the race and would have a hard job before they got back.

At the same time they were full of admiration for Amundsen, and were glad that, at any rate, men of both nations had per-

SELF-SACRIFICE

formed the difficult job of getting to the Pole.

Thenceforward it was a desperate job for them to work their way back over the 900 miles that lay between them and the base camp. Had the weather favoured them, they could just have managed it, picking up food supplies which they had cached on the outward journey.

But the weather did not favour them. Blizzards and snowstorms prevented them getting along. Week after week they fought their way. Food ran short; one after another they suffered from frost-bite. At last Evans fell, and suffered concussion and died.

They pressed on and dragged on till they had no food left, and though they had only eleven miles to go to reach the next store of

PADDLE YOUR OWN CANOE

food, violent storms of icy killing wind and snow stopped them where they were.

Then it was that Oates did his never-to-be-forgotten act of self-sacrifice.

His feet were frost-bitten. He knew that even if he could struggle on he would only delay his comrades. If he dropped out it would be one less mouth to feed and they might just have a chance of reaching the next depot.

So he crept from their little tent into the blinding blizzard and—dropped out.

He was never seen again. He gave his life that his comrades might live.

Unfortunately Oates' heroic self-sacrifice did not

The Statue of Captain Scott by Lady Scott

SELF-SACRIFICE

after all save his comrades. Starved and frozen they all died together. There they were found some months later by a search party, all lying as if asleep in their tent.

Captain Scott had kept a diary of their doings from day to day, so the whole history of the great trek is known. He wrote at the end—

"We shall stick it out to the end but we are getting weaker of course and the end cannot be far off. It seems a pity but I don't think I can write more."

In a letter also he wrote:

"We are weak. Writing is difficult. For my own sake I do not regret this journey which has shown that Englishmen can endure hardships, help one another, and meet death with as great fortitude as ever in the past."

Remember those words and Be Prepared if ever it should be necessary, to do as Oates

PADDLE YOUR OWN CANOE and Scott and those brave comrades of theirs did—to endure hardships, help one another, and meet death bravely—not caring for your own safety so long as you are carrying out your duty.

THE END

www.ingramcontent.com/pod-product-compliance
Lightning Source LLC
Chambersburg PA
CBHW031711230426
43668CB00006B/182